I Love Reading

Level 1

by
Theresa Gerig
Kris Robinson-Cobb
Glenda S. Shull

Published by Instructional Fair
an imprint of
Frank Schaffer Publications®

Frank Schaffer Publications®

Send all inquiries to:
Frank Schaffer Publications
8720 Orion Place
Columbus, OH 43240

I Love Reading—grade 1

ISBN 1-56822-826-0

3 4 5 6 7 8 9 PAT 11 10 09 08 07

Table of Contents

© 2006 Frank Schaffer Publications   1-56822-826-0

Ben's Leaves

Ben got a rake from the house. He raked the red and yellow leaves. He raked them into a big pile. He called his friends Matt and Sarah. The three friends jumped into the big pile.

1-56822-826-0

Choose words from the story to answer
the questions.

1. Where did Ben get the rake? _____

    _____

    _____

2. What did Ben do with the rake? _____

    _____

3. Who are Ben's friends? _____

    _____

4. Why did Ben call his friends? _____

    _____

5. How else could the children use the

    leaves? _____

    _____

    _____

1-56822-826-0

5

At the Zoo

Lee went to a place with many animals. He stopped to look at one little animal. It was black and white. The animal was in the water. It swam up and down very fast. Then the animal hopped out of the water. It walked with a funny little walk. On the land there were many other animals like it. What animal did Lee see?

1-56822-826-0

Draw a circle around the animal Lee saw.

Read the beginning of each sentence. Draw a line to the correct ending.

The animal   can swim.
                                     can fly.

The animal is   at the farm.
                                     at the zoo.

The animal   is alive.
                                     is a toy.

1-56822-826-0

Bedtime

Fuzzy Bear and I can't sleep.

"Let's go **under** the bed," I said. But it was too dark.

"Let's go **behind** the bed," I said. But it was too crowded.

"Let's jump **on top** of the bed," I said. But it was too bouncy.

"Let's lie down **in** the bed, just for a while."

"Good night, Fuzzy Bear."

 1-56822-826-0

Rewrite these words under the correct pictures.

under	behind	on top	in

_____

_____

_____

_____

Draw a bed just for Fuzzy Bear. Draw Fuzzy

Bear **under** the bed.

1-56822-826-0

Fly, Fly Away

The little baby spider climbed up to the top of the leaf. Then he let out a long strand of silk. The wind turned the silk into a balloon and lifted the spider away! Bye-bye baby spider!

1-56822-826-0

Use 1, 2, 3, and 4 to number the pictures in story order.

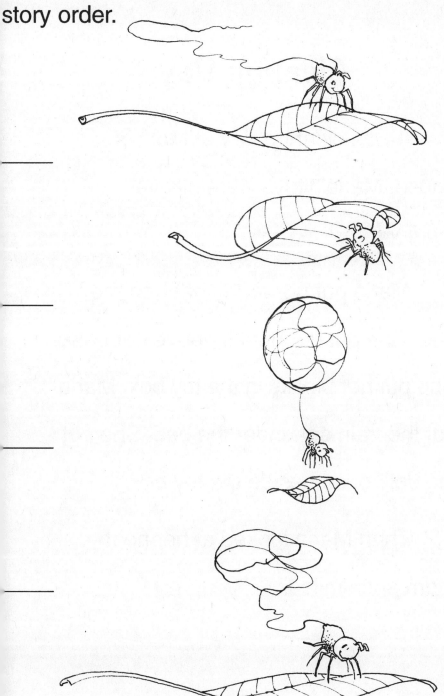

Cleanup Day

It was cleanup day at Maria's house. Maria's toys were all over the floor.

Maria put her teddy bear on the bed. She put her books above her desk. She put her blocks in the toy box. Maria put the train set under the bed. She put the dollhouse beside the toy box.

Then Maria looked at her neat room and smiled.

1-56822-826-0

Glue each toy in place to show where Maria put it.

1-56822-826-0

13

Kittens

Mother Cat watched her four kittens jump out of their box. The gray kitten chased a butterfly. The black kitten played with Mother Cat's tail. The spotted kitten jumped after a grasshopper. The yellow kitten played with the girl. Later, four tired kittens napped in the box.

1-56822-826-(

Color the kittens to match the story.

Circle the correct ending to each sentence.

1. Mother Cat had

   three kittens.

   four kittens.

2. The kittens

   looked just like their mother.

   were different colors.

3. The gray kitten

   chased a butterfly.

   jumped after a grasshopper.

1-56822-826-0

Riddle Time

Read each clue. Circle the correct answer.
Draw a picture with all the details.

1. I have four sides and four corners. All of my sides are the same size. What shape am I?
   circle
   square
   triangle

2. I live in water and I live on land. I have four legs and a tail. I hide inside my shell when I get scared. Who am I?
   frog
   snail
   turtle

3. You can go from place to place in me. You sit inside of me. I can go fast or I can go slow. I am in the water. What am I?
   boat
   car
   skis

1-56822-826-(

4. Tyler sits at his desk. He sits next to Troy,
    Wendy, and Isabel. He listens to Miss Henry.
    Then he writes his numbers. Where is
    Tyler?
    home
    library
    school

5. Missy puts on her coat, mittens, and hat.
    She takes her sled outside to play. She slides
    down the big white hill. What season is it?
    fall
    winter
    summer

6. Mom packed the food. Dad packed the
    tent. Cory packed the sleeping bags and a
    teddy bear. What is the family going to do?
    camp
    go to the lake
    hike

© 2006 Frank Schaffer Publications   1-56822-826-0

17

What Season?

Read each story about Grandmother and Kyler. Mark the season. Draw a picture of the activity.

1. Grandmother and Kyler put on coats, hats, gloves, and boots. They went outside to make a snowman.

    ○ spring

    ○ winter

    ○ summer

    ○ fall

2. Grandmother and Kyler were hot. They played in the water. They built a sand castle.

    ○ spring

    ○ winter

    ○ summer

    ○ fall

1-56822-826-0

3. Grandmother and Kyler worked in the garden. They planted corn, beans, and lettuce.

○ spring

○ winter

○ summer

○ fall

4. Grandmother and Kyler walked through the yellow and red leaves. They raked them into a pile.

○ spring

○ winter

○ summer

○ fall

© 2006 Frank Schaffer Publications

1-56822-826-0

19

Four Short Stories

After reading each story, fill in the circle next to the main idea.

1. A Day at the Beach

Alisha and Selena had fun at the beach. Alisha made a big sand castle. Selena made paper cup boats. They covered each other with sand. They played in the water. They did not want to go home.

◯ They did not want to go home.

◯ Alisha and Selena had fun at the beach.

◯ They played in the water.

2. Mother's Helper

Kim helped Mother. Kim cleaned her room. She put her clean socks away. Kim set the dishes on the table for dinner. Mother washed the dishes. Kim dried the dishes. They talked about working together.

◯ Kim set the dishes on the table.

◯ Kim cleaned her room.

◯ Kim helped Mother.

1-56822-826-(

3. At the Zoo

Ben and Troy visited the city zoo. The bears and lions were asleep. Troy fed peanuts to an elephant. The boys watched a hippo take a bath. Ben rode a pony. They petted bunnies at the petting zoo.

○ Ben and Troy visited the city zoo.

○ Ben rode a pony.

○ They petted bunnies at the petting zoo.

4. In the Garden

Brad and Jeff worked in the garden. First, they pulled all the weeds. Then, Brad planted corn. Jeff planted beans. Then, they watered the plants and seeds.

○ Jeff planted beans.

○ They watered the plants.

○ Brad and Jeff worked in the garden.

The Watsons

The Watsons needed milk from the store.

So the family rushed out the door.

The Watsons drove to town.

On the way they saw a clown.

The clown had a cat.

The cat was in a hat.

The clown had a dog.

The dog sat on a log.

The clown had a goat.

The goat was in a coat.

The Watsons laughed at the silly clown.

They forgot why they had come to town.

  1-56822-826-0

Read the word above each car. Find the word in the story that rhymes. Write it in the car.

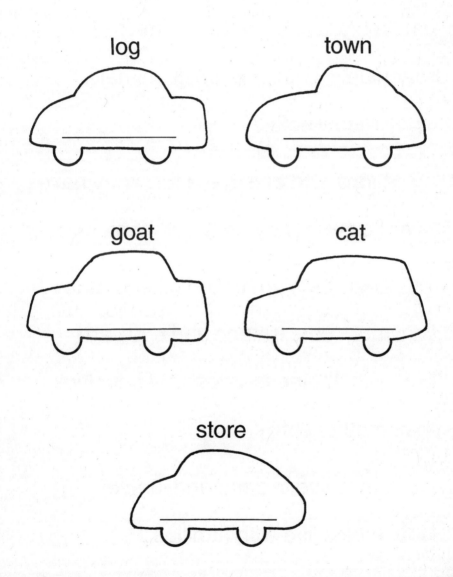

log

town

goat

cat

store

1-56822-826-0

23

The Big Cat Family

Lions and house cats belong in the cat family. Lions are big animals. They roar loudly. Cats are small animals. They meow softly.

Lions and cats have fur. They have sharp claws. They are good hunters.

Baby cats are called kittens. Baby lions are cubs. Kittens and cubs are born with their eyes closed. They drink their mother's milk.

Lions live in zoos and jungles. House cats live with families.

© 2006 Frank Schaffer Publications
1-56822-826-0

Read the facts. Color the lion's paw if the fact is about lions. Color the cat's paw if the fact is about house cats. Color both paws if the fact is about both.

roar loudly

are small animals

belong in the cat family

have fur

babies are called cubs

born with their eyes closed

drink their mother's milk

live with families

1-56822-826-0

In the Snow

It was snowing. The girls were bored. Lydia said, "I have a plan." Lee and Sandy liked her plan.

The girls rolled some snow into a big ball. Then they rolled a second snowball. They set the second snowball on top of the first snowball. Then they rolled a third snowball and set it on top of the second ball.

Sandy went into her house. She came out with a carrot and some buttons. Lee found an old hat, some mittens, and a broom. Lydia picked up two sticks by the tree.

The girls clapped. They had made

a _____ .

1-56822-826-C

Draw a picture of the thing that Lydia,
Lee, and Sandy created in the snow.
Include all the details from the story.

1-56822-826-0

27

Purrty's Kittens

Purrty has two kittens. Purrty's kittens are not alike. One kitten is named Big. One kitten is named Little. Big is white. Little is black. Big has long hair. Little has short hair. Big plays in high places. Little plays in low places. Big moves fast. Little moves slowly. Big sleeps in the box. Little sleeps outside of the box. Big plays in the day. Little plays at night. Purrty's kittens are alike in one way. Big likes milk and Little likes milk.

1-56822-826-0

In the story: Underline in red the words that describe Big. Underline in blue the words that describe Little.

Match the opposites.

day	big
little	white
black	night
long	low
fast	short
high	out
in	slow

2006 Frank Schaffer Publications

1-56822-826-0

Going Fishing

Marty and her grandpa love to go fishing on Sundays. There are five lakes in their county. The lakes have different kinds of fish.

Map Key

sunfish   bass

bluegill   catfish

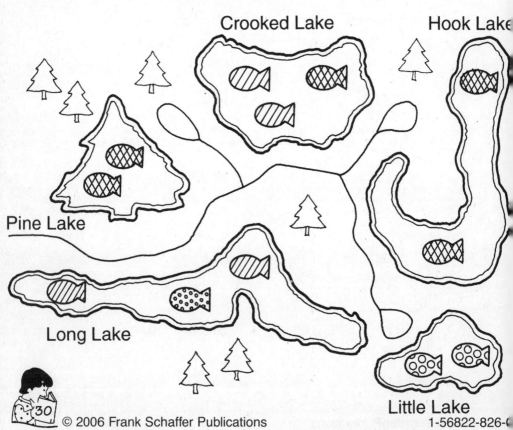

Crooked Lake

Hook Lake

Pine Lake

Long Lake

Little Lake

1-56822-826-0

Look at the map of Fish Country. Answer the
questions about the map.

1. Marty and Grandpa want to catch
   catfish. In which lake should they fish?

   _____

2. They want to catch bass. To which lakes
   could they go? _____

   _____

3. Which lake has bluegill in it?

   _____

4. Marty and Grandpa want to catch sunfish.
   Where should they fish?

   _____ _____

5. Which lake has bluegill and sunfish?

   _____

6. Grandpa wants to cook sunfish and bass for
   dinner. In which lake should they fish?

   _____

Happy Birthday
Baby Bear

It was Baby Bear's first birthday. When Mother Bear opened the door, Baby Bear's friends shouted, "Surprise!"

The animals sang "Happy Birthday" to Baby Bear. Betty Bee gave Baby Bear some honey. Sammy Squirrel gave Baby Bear some nuts. Randy Raccoon gave Baby Bear some fish. Sally Skunk gave Baby Bear some bugs. Freddy Frog gave Baby Bear cold water from the spring. Mother Bear gave all the friends birthday cake. They had a fun time at the birthday party.

1-56822-826-

Finish the notes about Baby Bear's birthday party.

The animals went _____

_____ .

The animals went there because _____

_____ .

List the gifts and who gave them.

_____

_____

_____

_____

_____

Mother Bear gave _____

_____ .

Trip to the Beach

The Brown family wanted to spend the whole day at the beach. They went to bed early. The alarm clock did not ring. The Browns slept all morning.

They started to drive to the beach. Mr. Brown forgot to put gas in the van. The van ran out of gas.

It was late afternoon. Big, dark clouds filled the sky. The Browns did not look happy.

Mr. Brown parked the van at the beach. A big raindrop fell on the window. It rained and rained. The Browns looked at the beach from inside their van.

1-56822-826-

Answer these questions about the Browns'
day at the beach.

1. Why did the Browns go to bed early?

   _____

   _____

2. Why did the Browns sleep all morning?

   _____

   _____

3. Why did the van run out of gas?

   _____

   _____

4. Why didn't the Browns look happy in the
   afternoon? _____

   _____

5. Why did the Browns stay inside the van at
   the beach? _____

   _____

© 2006 Frank Schaffer Publications 1-56822-826-0 35

Duck's Busy Week

On Sunday, Duck walked to the park. She played with friends and swam in the pond. The next day, she baked bread and went for a swim in her pool.

On Tuesday, it rained. Duck cleaned her house and went for a walk in the rain. The rain made her feathers feel soft. The next day, Duck washed her clothes and called her friend Rabbit.

On Thursday, Duck planted a flower garden and swam in her pool. The next day, she went to town to do her shopping.

On Saturday, she took a shower and visited her grandmother. Duck told her grandmother all about her busy week.

36

1-56822-826-

Pretend you are Duck. Write about each day in your journal.

Sunday _____

_____

Monday _____

_____

Tuesday _____

_____

Wednesday _____

_____

Thursday _____

_____

Friday _____

_____

Saturday _____

_____

  1-56822-826-0

Candy-Bar Contest

The three friends opened their candy-bar wrappers. There was a contest inside. What prizes did they win?

Randy's wrapper said, "Sorry, please try again." He threw his wrapper on the ground. He stepped on it. "It's try again, try again, every time," he yelled.

Nikki jumped for joy. Her wrapper said, "You're a winner! Good for one free candy bar." Nikki shouted, "I've never won before!"

Robert read his wrapper. He said, "It would have been nice to win. I guess I'll just have try again." He put the wrapper in a trash can.

1-56822-826-C

Write the names of the
children beside the faces
that show how they feel.
Below the faces, write if
they feel sad, surprised,
or mad.

_____

_____

_____

_____

_____

_____

More

Marcus had an old, blue truck. He wanted a new, red truck. Mom bought him a new truck. But Marcus wasn't happy.

Marcus had an old, fuzzy teddy bear. He wanted a new, talking bear. Dad bought him a new bear. But Marcus wasn't happy.

Marcus had old, yellow blocks. He wanted new, wooden blocks. Grandma bought him new blocks. But he still wasn't happy.

Marcus took his new toys to the park. He saw a sad boy playing alone. Marcus shared his toys with the sad boy. The boy smiled. Marcus was happy.

 1-56822-826-

Draw a line from the question to the
correct answer.

1. Why did Marcus
   want a red truck?

2. Why did Dad buy a
   new bear?

3. What happened
   when Marcus got
   new toys?

4. Why did the boy
   smile?

5. Why was Marcus
   happy at the end of
   the story?

A. Marcus wanted
   a talking bear.

B. Marcus shared
   his toys with him.

C. Marcus wasn't
   happy.

D. He had an old,
   blue truck.

E. He had made the
   little boy happy.

Kandy

Kandy put white makeup on her face. She painted on big, red, smiling lips. She painted blue star shapes around her eyes. She placed a big red ball on her small nose. She blew up two long balloons. She twisted them to make a hat. She put the hat over her rainbow-colored wig. Kandy looked in the mirror and laughed at herself. Her feet flopped out the door. She walked to the children's floor at the hospital.

1-56822-826-C

Answer the questions below.

1. What is Kandy?

   _____

2. What were the clues that helped you?

   _____

   _____

   _____

   _____

3. Why do you think Kandy's feet flopped?

   _____

   _____

4. Why did Kandy go to the hospital?

   _____

   _____

The Puzzle

Tito and Ann were putting together a farm puzzle. Tito left the room to answer the phone. His little sister finished the puzzle.

Tito looked at the puzzle and began to laugh. Ann had put the rooster head on the cow body. She had put the horse head on the pig body. She had put the cow head on the horse body. She had put the pig head on the rooster body.

Tito sat down with Ann. He read her a book about farm animals. After they finished the book, Tito and Ann put the farm animals together the right way.

1-56822-826-(

Match the bodies and heads as Ann did first.

Match the bodies and heads as Ann and Tito did after reading.

1-56822-826-0

45

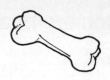

The Pet Store

Trent and his dad looked in the pet store window. Trent pointed at something. Dad said, "Oh, isn't that cute?"

They went into the store. Trent picked out a water bowl, collar, and leash. Dad picked out a chew bone and a bag of food. Then they asked the store owner for help. They led him to the store window. Trent pointed at the thing they wanted. The store owner reached into the pen and picked it up.

1-56822-826-0

Read the story and answer the questions.

1. What do you think was in the pen in the window?

    _____

2. What words helped you know what animal it was?

    _____

    _____

3. What do you think will happen next?

    _____

    _____

1-56822-826-0   47

The Game

Kim, Dan, Ann, and Bob were playing cards. Kim said, "Let's play one more game. The winner of this game will be named the best card player of all." The children agreed.

Suddenly Bob yelled, "I win."

"Wow, that's a surprise," Kim said.

"I wanted to be the best," said Dan. He started to cry.

"That's not fair. You didn't even win any of the other games!" Ann yelled. She threw her cards down.

Bob smiled at the others. "I'm the best card player." he said.

© 2006 Frank Schaffer Publications 1-56822-826-0

Write the names of the children beside the faces that show how they feel. Below the faces, write if they feel happy, sad, mad, or surprised.

Word Bank

Dan   sad
Kim   surprised
Ann   mad
Bob   happy

 _____

_____

 _____

_____

 _____

_____

 _____

_____

    1-56822-826-0

Jodi's Cars

Jody found a box at her grandma's house. The box held lots of toy cars. She dumped the cars out on the floor. Jodi put the cars in lines. Each line of cars was a different color.

Jodi had a line with six yellow cars. She had four blue cars. She had seven red cars. She had five green cars. Jodi made another line. In it she put one black car, one orange car, and one brown car.

Then she turned the box upside down and made a garage. She parked the cars in the garage.

1-56822-826-C

Color the cars like Jodi arranged them.

Write the color and number words from the story.

Color Words	Number Words

1-56822-826-0

The Balloons

The Mouse family had a fun day at the circus. The Mouse children saw a clown with balloons.

"We want balloons." the children cried. "Please, Mom, please." Mother Mouse bought seven balloons. Each balloon was a different color. "I want red." "No, I want red," the children all cried.

Mother Mouse looked at her jumping, crying children. "Each of you will get the best balloon for you," she said. She gave blue to Sue, green to Arleen, black to Mack, gray to Tray, white to Bright, and yellow to Fellow. The red balloon was still in her hand. She gave it to Mr. Mouse and said, "Red for Fred."

1-56822-826-C

Color the balloons to show what each mouse got.

Tray

Bright

Fellow

Sue

Fred

Arleen

Mack

1-56822-826-0

Teacher's Surprise

Dan walked to school each day. On the way, he liked to find things to give his teacher. Dan liked Miss Read. She always smiled when he gave her something he had found.

Today, Dan saw something that he knew Miss Read would like. He picked it from a tree. He put the red object in his lunch pail. Dan stepped inside the school. He walked to Miss Read's desk and handed her the gift. Miss Read smiled and said, "Thank you, Dan. I'll enjoy it with my lunch."

1-56822-826-

Answer the questions in complete sentences.

1. What did Dan find? _____

_____

2. What will Miss Read do with the surprise?

_____

3. What other things do you think Dan found
   and gave to Miss Read?

_____

_____

_____

1-56822-826-0

55

The Bicycle

It was my birthday. I blew out the candles on my cake. My mom and dad brought out my gift. It was a bicycle. It was just what I wanted. It was blue with silver handlebars. It had a red horn and a light.

I put on my helmet and went for a ride. I rode up and down the hills. I honked the horn at my friends. I turned on the light. I looked both ways for cars and trucks. I walked my bike across the street.

 1-56822-826-

Draw a picture in each box to show what is missing from the story.

It was my birthday. I blew out the [ ]

on my [ ]. My mom and dad brought out

my [ ]. It was a [ ]. It was just what I

wanted. It was blue with silver [ ]. It had a

red [ ] and a [ ].

I put on my [ ] and went for a ride. I

rode up and down the [ ]. I honked the

horn at my [ ]. I turned on the [ ].

looked both ways for [ ] and [ ].

walked my bike across the [ ].

Boots and Tony

Boots is Tony's puppy. Tony and Boots like to run and play at the park. One day, Tony climbed the jungle gym. Boots could not see Tony. Boots ran and ran looking for Tony.

Boots stopped running. He asked a bird, "Where am I?"

The bird said, "You are on Oak Street. What street do you live on?" Boots did not know the name of his street. "You are lost," said the bird.

Boots cried, "Tony is lost too."

The bird said, "Who is Tony?"

"Tony is my boy who takes me to the park."

The bird said, "There are many boys named Tony. That does not help. I know my

1-56822-826

way to the park. Follow me."

Boots followed the bird to the park. Boots saw Tony. Tony was yelling, "Here, Boots. Where are you, Boots?"

Answer these questions.

1. Why did the bird say Boots was lost?

_____

_____

2. Why did knowing Tony's name not help the bird? _____

_____

3. Why do you think Tony was yelling for Boots? _____

_____

4. If you get lost, what are some things you should know? _____

_____

_____

_____

Best Friends

Kara and Sara are best friends.

They are seven years old.

They are neighbors.

They are best friends.

The friends have brown hair.

Kara's hair is curly.

Sara's hair is straight.

They are best friends.

The friends have green eyes.

Sara wears glasses,

But Kara doesn't.

They are best friends.

The friends like to laugh and talk.

They tell each other stories.

They say, "We will always be best friends."

1-56822-826-

Tell how Kara and Sara are alike.

_____

_____

_____

_____

_____

Tell how Kara and Sara are different.

_____

_____

_____

_____

_____

1-56822-826-0

Jan's Pony

Jan lives in the country. She asked for a pony. Her parents said she must learn how to care for a pony first. Jan read books about ponies. She talked to friends who had ponies. Jan listed seven rules about caring for a pony.

Rules

1. A pony needs a clean, dry stall.

2. It needs a large area outside to get exercise.

3. A pony eats grain and hay twice daily.

4. A pony must have clean water to drink.

5. The pony must be brushed every day.

6. A veterinarian should visit the pony yearly.

1-56822-826-0

7. Its hooves must be picked clean of

stones every day.

   Jan's parents read the list. Caring for a

pony is a lot of work. Jan still wanted a pony.

Soon they began shopping for a pony.

What must Jan's family have before she gets
the pony? _____

_____

_____

What does a pony need every day?

_____

_____

_____

What must happen every year? _____

_____

Plants and People

Plants are important to people. People eat plants. Foods such as apples, bananas, potatoes, and peas come from plants. Even the flours for bread and cereal come from plants.

Meats do not come from plants. Milk and eggs do not come from plants. They come from animals. But the animals eat plants. Plants are important to people.

1-56822-826-(

Finish the sentences with words from the story.

1. Apples and potatoes come from

   _____ .

2. Flour comes from _____ .

3. Meats come from _____ .

4. Animals eat _____ .

Write two sentences that tell why plants are
important to people.

_____

_____

_____

_____

_____

_____

_____

1-56822-826-0

65

The Smartest Dog

I have a new puppy. Her name is Lady. She is a collie. My puppy is brown, black, and white. Lady was the prettiest dog at the pet store.

Lady is small now. She is up to my knees. She will grow to be the biggest dog in town.

My puppy is the smartest dog. She knows her name. She plays fetch.

1-56822-826-(

Color the bone red if the sentence is a fact.

Color the bone blue if the sentence is an opinion.

Lady is a collie.

Lady is brown, black, and white.

Lady was the prettiest dog at the pet store.

Lady is small. She is up to my knees.

Lady will be the biggest dog.

Lady plays fetch.

Lady is the smartest dog.

1-56822-826-0

A-a-a-choo!

What do you think happens when you sneeze?

_____

_____

What would you like to know about a sneeze?

_____

_____

    Anyone can sneeze at anytime. It may happen when you are sick with a cold. You may have an allergy. Or sometimes there is nothing wrong with you at all.

    It all begins in your nose. Your nose has lots and lots of tiny hairs inside of it. The hairs help

1-56822-826-0

clean the air that you breathe. The hairs

catch dust and other things so they don't go

into your lungs.

Sneezing is good for you. It rids your

nose of dust and germs. Your sneeze can be

harmful to others. Germs fly out of your

mouth and nose. These germs can make

other people sick. So be sure to cover your

mouth and nose when you get ready to sn-

sn-sneeze!

Why do people sneeze? _____

_____

_____

_____

© 2006 Frank Schaffer Publications   1-56822-826-0

69

How Long?

This chart is about animals that are taken care of by people. These animals have a safe home, good food, and room to run and play, too.

Did you know that a mouse lives about two years? Some animals live much longer. Read the chart to see how long these animals live.

Animals	How long do they live?	Homes
mouse	2 years	house
dog	13 years	house
cat	14 years	house
cow	25 years	farm
pig	25 years	farm
elephant	60 years	zoo
land tortoise	100 years	zoo

70

1-56822-826-

Read the chart and answer the questions.

How long does an elephant live?_____

How long does a cow live?_____

Which lives longer?   a cow   a dog

Which lives longer?   a cat   a mouse

Which two animals live the same number of
years?

_____   _____

Which animal lives the longest?

_____

2006 Frank Schaffer Publications   1-56822-826-0

Rainbows

After it rains, you may see a rainbow. A rainbow is made when sunlight shines through water drops. The rainbow is made of the colors of light.

The rainbow's colors are always in the same order. Red is on the top of the rainbow. Orange and yellow follow red. Next we see green. Blue comes next. Purple is the color on the bottom.

1-56822-826-

Color the rainbow with colors in the correct order.

2006 Frank Schaffer Publications   1-56822-826-0

What do you know about the sun? _____

_____

What would you like to know about the sun?

_____

_____

The Sun

The bright light in the sky is the sun. The sun is a big star that gives off light. We see the sun during the day. Sunlight can shine through clouds. Never look right at the sun. It can hurt your eyes.

The sun gives off heat. We can't see heat but we can feel it. Think about playing outside on a sunny day. Your skin feels the heat from the sun.

     1-56822-826-

Sunlight helps plants to grow. Plants make food in their leaves. They must have the light and heat from the sun to do this. Without the sun, most plants die.

Our sun is important to all of us. We use the sun every day. Enjoy the sun!

_____

What did you learn about the sun? _____

_____

_____

_____

_____

_____

_____

_____

 1-56822-826-0 75

Answer Key

Ben's Leaves

1. He got the rake from the house.
2. Ben raked the leaves into a pile.
3. Ben's friends are Matt and Sarah.
4. He called his friends to jump in the big pile.
5. Answers will vary.

page 5

At the Zoo

Circle the penguin.
1. The animal can swim.
2. The animal is at the zoo.
3. The animal is alive.

page 7

Bedtime

behind   in
under   on top

page 9

Fly, Fly, Away

2
1
4
3

page 11

Cleanup Day

page 13

Kittens

1. Mother Cat had four kittens.
2. The kittens were different colors.
3. The gray kitten chased a butterfly.

page 15

Riddle Time

1. square
2. turtle
3. boat
4. school
5. winter
6. camp

pages 16–17

What Season?

1. winter
2. summer
3. spring
4. fall

pages 18–19

Four Short Stories

1. Alisha and Selena had fun at the beach.
2. Kim helped Mother.
3. Ben and Troy visited the city zoo.
4. Brad and Jeff worked in the garden.

pages 20–21

     1-56822-826

The Watsons

log	**town**
dog	clown
goat	**cat**
coat	hat

store
door

page 23

The Big Cat Family

 roar loudly

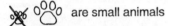 are small animals

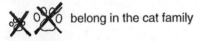 belong in the cat family

 have fur

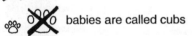 babies are called cubs

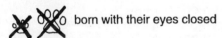 born with their eyes closed

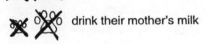 drink their mother's milk

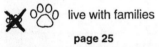 live with families

page 25

In the Snow

The picture should be a snowman made of three balls of snow. The snowman has a carrot nose, a hat, stick arms, mittens, and a broom.

page 27

Purrty's Kittens

Underline in red: day, big, long, fast, high, in, white

Underline in blue: little, black, night, low, short, out, slow

day–night	fast–slow
little–big	high–low
black–white	in–out
long–short	

page 29

Going Fishing

1. Little Lake
2. Pine Lake and Hook Lake
3. Long Lake
4. Crooked Lake or Long Lake
5. Long Lake
6. Crooked Lake

page 31

Happy Birthday Baby Bear

The animals went to Baby Bear's house.

The animals went there because it was his birthday and there was a party.

honey–Betty Bee
nuts–Sammy Squirrel
fish–Randy Raccoon
bugs–Sally Skunk
cold water–Freddy Frog

Mother Bear gave all the friends birthday cake.

page 33

Trip to the Beach

1. They wanted to spend the whole day at the beach.
2. The alarm clock did not ring.
3. Mr. Brown forgot to put gas in the van.
4. It looked like it might rain.
5. It rained at the beach.

page 35

Duck's Busy Week

Student journals will vary, but should include the events from the story.

page 37

Candy-Bar Contest

mad–Randy

surprised–Nikki

sad–Robert

page 39

More

1. D
2. A
3. C
4. B
5. E

page 41

Kandy

1. a clown
2. white makeup, big, red lips, red ball on her nose, ballon hat, rainbow-colored wig, floppy feet, blue stars
3. Her shoes were too big.
4. She was probably going to entertain the sick children with a clown act.

page 43

The Puzzle

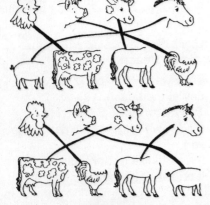

page 45

The Pet Store

1. a dog
2. water bowl, collar, leash, chew bone, and pen
3. Trent and his dad will probably take the dog home and play with it.

page 47

The Game

Ann–mad	Kim–surprised
Bob–happy	Dan–sad

page 49

Jodi's Cars

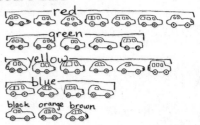

Color Words	Number Words
yellow	six
blue	four
red	seven
green	five
black	one
orange	
brown	

page 51

The Balloons

Fellow–yellow	Tray–gray
Bright–white	Arleen–green
Mack–black	Fred–red
Sue–blue	

page 53

Teacher's Surprise

1. Dan found an apple.
2. She will eat it with her lunch.
3. Answers will vary.

page 55

 1-56822-826-(

The Bicycle

It was my birthday. I blew out the [image]
on my [cake]. My mom and dad brought out
my [present]. It was a [bicycle]. It was just what I
wanted. It was blue with silver [image]. It had a
red [image] and a [image].
I put on my [helmet] and went for a ride. I
rode up and down the [hills]. I honked the
horn at my [friends]. I turned on the [light].
I looked both ways for [cars] and [truck].
I walked my bike across the [crosswalk].

page 57

Boots and Tony

1. Boots could not tell the bird the name of his street.
2. There are many boys named Tony. The bird did not know which one Boots was talking about.
3. Tony thought Boots was lost. He hoped that Boots would hear him calling and come running back.
4. Answers will vary. Answers may include your last name, your address, your phone number, and your parents' names.

page 59

Best Friends

Alike:
They are both seven years old. They are neighbors. They both have brown hair and green eyes. They like to laugh and talk. They both tell stories.
Different:
Kara's hair is curly and Sara's is straight. Sara wears glasses and Kara doesn't.

page 61

Jan's Pony

Jan's family must have a stall and a large outside area for exercising the pony.

Every day, the pony needs to eat grain and hay and drink clean water. The pony must be brushed and have its hooves picked clean of stones every day.

Every year, a veterinarian should visit the pony.

page 63

Plants and People

1. Apples and potatoes come from **plants.**
2. Flour comes from **plants.**
3. Meats come from **animals.**
4. Animals eat **plants.**

Sentences will vary.

page 65

The Smartest Dog

Lady is a collie. (red fact)

Lady is brown, black, and white. (red fact)

Lady was the prettiest dog at the pet store. (blue opinion)

Lady is small. She is up to my knees. (red fact)

Lady will be the biggest dog. (blue opinion)

Lady plays fetch. (red fact)

Lady is the smartest dog. (blue opinion)

page 67

A-a-a-choo!

Predictions at the beginning of the article will vary.

Why do people sneeze? They sneeze when they have a cold or when the hairs in their noses catch dust and germs that shouldn't go in their lungs.

page 69

How Long?

An elephant lives 60 years.
A cow lives 25 years.
A cow lives longer than a dog.
A cat lives longer than a mouse.
Cows and pigs both live 25 years.
The land tortoise lives the longest of these animals listed.

page 71

Rainbows

The correct order from the top:
red
orange
yellow
green
blue
purple.

page 73

The Sun

Predictions at the beginning of the article will vary.

What did you learn about the sun? The sun is a big star. The sun can hurt your eyes if you look directly at it. The sun provides heat and light. Sunlight helps plants to grow. Without the sun, plants will die.

page 75

     1-56822-826-